salmonpoetry

Diverse Voices from Ireland and the World

the **arts** council an chomhairle ealaíon

funding **literature**

Word Skin
Orla Fay

Published in 2023 by
Salmon Poetry
Cliffs of Moher, County Clare, Ireland
Website: www.salmonpoetry.com
Email: info@salmonpoetry.com

ISBN 978-1-915022-43-1

Cover Image: SarapulSar38 – istockphoto
Cover Design & Typesetting: *Siobhán Hutson Jeanotte*

Printed in Ireland by Sprint Print

Salmon Poetry gratefully acknowledges the support of
The Arts Council / An Chomhairle Ealaíon

"Though I am often in the depths of misery, there is still calmness, pure harmony and music inside me. I see paintings or drawings in the poorest cottages, in the dirtiest corners. And my mind is driven towards these things with an irresistible momentum... Poetry surrounds us everywhere, but putting it on paper is, alas, not so easy as looking at it. I dream my painting, and then I paint my dream."

VINCENT VAN GOGH

Acknowledgements

Thanks to the editors of the following publications or websites in which some of the poems, or versions of the poems, first appeared: *An Anthology of Reactions, Boyne Berries, Clear Poetry, Crossways Literary Magazine, Dodging the Rain, Fingal Libraries, Hold Open the Door, Honest Ulsterman, Live Encounters, Meath Writers' Circle Annual Magazine, New Poems of Oriel, Poethead, Poetry Ireland Review, Poetry Porch, Quarryman, Red Lines, ROPES, Skylight 47, Southword, Spontaneity, Stepaway Magazine, Tales from the Forest, The Galway Review, The Irish Times, The Lake, The Ofi Press, The Ogham Stone, The Stony Thursday Book*; and to the judges and organisers of the following competitions in which poems were either ranked or shortlisted: Anthony Cronin, Cúirt, Dermot Healy, Fingal Libraries Travels with Joyce, Francis Ledwidge, Meath County Library Éist Poetry Competition, Jonathan Swift and Red Line.

Thanks to the members of Boyne Writers Group: Michael Farry, Paddy Smith, Barbara Flood, Anne Crinion, Tom Dredge, Sinéad MacDevitt, Frances Browne, and to Frank Murphy of Meath Writers' Circle. Thanks to poets and friends in the wider writing community.

Thanks to my parents, Christy and Eilish, and to my brothers, sister and family. Thank you to my friends. Thank you, Sarah.

Thanks to Jessie Lendennie, Siobhán Hutson Jeanotte and Dani Gill at Salmon Poetry.

Contents

I. *Fields*

II. *Beyond Caravaggio*

I. Fields

A Thaw in Time

for Tara

When the world becomes sparse
the red berries among the spoils
come to the foreground.

Her words tumble out
as quickly as she thinks
and the ice suddenly melts

in a blast of sunlight.
Relaying what I had told her,
my words are taken as grave truth;

the little bird had hopped along the fence
pecking berries, filling its belly
for the winter

and she, just three years old,
danced in mirth with tangled curls
in the power of the words,

making me wonder if I had been like that myself.

Calibos takes Andromeda from her sleep

The Clash of the Titans, 1981

The steel playground slide collects at its base
rainwater that is warm as a pool
of seawater in the sunlight
left over by the tide.

Lush green trees are heavy with hawthorn,
perfect pearl throws.
On the electricity pole
the single crow
on a corner of wire that forms a square,
the north, the south, the east and the west.

The swallows dive pulling heart chariots;
theatrical daredevils.
The sky vacantly journeys aided by twilight
and abetted by the moon.

In the middle of the night, I awaken
to scurrying sounds that rise up
from below through the open window.
"Who is it?" the owl calls. "What do you want?"

Paralysis starts in the feet, travels
upwards coldly gripping calves.
Tumbling through darkness
I disturb fixed stars that startled
fall in glitter showers

in a world where trees drag their roots
across the swamp,
where voices are echoes,
where he fawns over his own reflection
in a pool adorned with vines

that are caressed by his arm's stump.
When the fire dawn birds call
I am picked up in talons
and returned to the cauldron of morning.

And I never remember who he was,
my captor, nor what he wanted
except that some dark part
of my soul questioned
and he answered.

Devil-may-care

The red moon rises
as the house of the sun sets.
Driving home from the sea in the dark
I am holding no one's hand.
I know this route so well.
I'm the child falling asleep in the backseat.
Mum censured the sea air.
One Sunday we made devil's food cake
and came to the strand.

Over the bridge now,
past the river and the abbey
the house of a late writer is in flames,
flames that lick the dusk sky
with smoke billowing upwards.
A crowd has gathered by a fire engine
at the crossroads.

I imagine she will always
be with me on these journeys
echoing forgotten, prophetic words,
my memory of her incombustible.
I'd come back for my notebooks,
the enchantment of words,
and the dogs, I'd come back for them.
If your house was burning
what would you take with you?

Seed and Spark

Failing to write a sunset poem
I gave up on Brooks, Teasdale and Lindsay,
falling to sleep in their colour,
mixing St. Louis' muddy water with French shale,
flint and sandstone.

When I woke in the morning I found
smouldering embers alive in the stove
and re-igniting the night's desire washed fresh,
so new, so clean I thought of Prometheus
and then my father, who had gone about
the dwindling light tending to the budding
apples and pears, wrapping them in fleeces
against the night's frost,
tender pookas looming
beneath the sown heavens
to frighten any moonlit passer-by –

Pluto descending to Hades and Proserpina
returning, clasping armfuls of daffodils
to her chest, whispering primrose promises,
naming each one *Pluto's Hidden Stars*.

The Natural Order

I start the year with care for what is small,
the black beetle caught in the threads of my glove,
warrior having survived the night,

experience the trauma in freeing him, or her, or it!
Ten minutes or more spent in surgery
and I never want to be a spider.

I suppose that yes there must be death,
that this is the universal law,
best make my peace with it now.

Yet I balked in finding fledglings on the roadside,
their tiny, almost weightless bodies
just not managing to fly,

how I lament
those who are this sacrifice,
the could-have-beens.

I ushered two to a leafy, grass and hedgerow
pyre, imagining that when the sun sets, or rises
the next day the cleansing by fire,

the ashes to ashes, dust to dust,
the earth giveth and taketh away, realise
that the great bounty of spring must have its casualties.

The murder of crows know this,
feeding on the freshly ploughed fields,
see that the land is life to their skies,

as do the worms, soil eaters and keepers know,
that the mother provides mealy moments
of subterranean artistry before the farmer's hand.

Fields

The fields that we knew are all gone:

The river field,
The hazel field
The pony field,
The middle field,
The big field,
The pump field,
The potato field,
The swamp field.

Thistles, wild roses, primroses,
daffodils, dandelions, daisies,
elderberry, ash, beech,
ragwort, nettle, dock leaf,
hawthorn, blackberry and sloe,
cooking apple and crab apple ago.

The bows and arrows,
the palatial pallet hut,
the kibbly lad, *
the barn's window ledge.

The hares at dawn,
the cows going home,
swallows in the gable,
bones of a dead animal.

The ghost of Jimmy Plunkett,
the horseshoe in the ditch,
the tar turned to liquorice.

The future in the distance –

is gone.

*a child's coined name for a squirrel

Caught in a Dance

In the morning their criss-cross serenade
on the field-top makes me the tickled-pink witness
to their knitted symmetry.

They fly so close that I could almost touch a wing tip
but I would be cut in the act so razor-like
are their dives and turns, so close-shaved.

The swallows weave me into this paired tapestry –
I could have been that single star flung out of space,
never to return to the darkness of the velvet sky.

I could have been shell-less carrion for the birds,
or that empty conch that craves perennially the return of the sea.
I might have thought that death was the metamorphosis of loneliness.

Looking-glass

Make me like the leaves in the distance
Dappled and far away and I will invent myself.

Oh you can never know me from the pieces of me,
Shattered glass of a mirror all over the floor

And who can tell of the true reflection then
That once was, never was, was lost – is!

Who can say but I looked at you too long,
Too long and you have no features,

I may have swallowed every part of you.
You are not there anymore. You disappeared.

There is nothing in not existing. You are dead.
But you don't know, do you? Do you know

That I'll feel a piece of glass that I swallowed
Cut and I'll see a reflection of myself

And it will be you I see, terribly true?
And I never knew, I never knew, I never knew.

Teenage Kicks, 1991-1996

The years I sat in the classroom
seem idyllic now, pre-boom
and aspiring the school's new wing;
the grey tables and chairs,
the green blackboard.
We opened the Book of History
as it had never been seen before,
on the Rising, The War of Independence,
Michael Collins, DeValera,
The Anglo-Irish Literary Revival,
W.B. Yeats and John Millington Synge.
We saw *The Playboy of the Western World*
in Trim's Town Hall Theatre
but all I could think of was the poetry;
the tattered copy of *Soundings*
that had been my brother's,
his inked-in hand-me-down notes
might cast some light on *The Fisherman*.

Rarely seen on the Boyne
the swan's repeat glimpsed lines
sewing time with their bills.
Still, I recall the wide-eyed wonder
of the *Lake Isle of Innisfree* at fifteen.
I look back and I would go back
but I cannot, Tír na nÓg, the
island across the waves –

The signatories, their names
once rhymed off without thought,
(Adorned the proclamation
hanging on the wall in the shoe shop
where the handsome boy lived
who played the Doors' *Break on Through*)
are now sought in bleached annals,
the sand of retreating tide,
dusted away chalk.

Blackberries

The blackberries are red when they are green,
fistfuls hanging by thorny bramble
and love's first flush is an unripened dream.

Once she was summer's wildest flower-queen
plucked by Romeo on woodland amble –
the blackberries are red when they are green

Untried and untested love was on-screen,
a kiss that faded to mere preamble
and love's first flush is an unripened dream

The Fall is magical when it's first seen,
with never an inkling of the gamble.
The blackberries are red when they are green.

The ending is always an unknown scene,
what pair do you pair from the ensemble
when love's first flush is an unripened dream?

Forever after is not libertine,
it is the taste of fruit full and ample.
The blackberries are red when they are green
and love's first flush is an unripened dream.

East of Eden

Autumn in the city of a thousand red lights
from afar a bed in the sapphire blue night
and I saw the ghost of James Dean pass my way,
smoke a cigarette just east of Eden.
And the moon could be rising
and we would be riding the stars
a million miles away,
far enough away to be alone,
to be solitary and blue like the night.
Blue like freedom.
I could take your hand in mine
walking through the stars,
the million stars,
the million pretty stars
and they'd never be as your eyes,
your far away eyes,
your eyes of a galaxy,
a distant place.
All your whispers would be light,
beams to trip the heart
and we would fall like heroes
into the city,
into the city like a bed,
an earthly paradise,
fly immortal
before the sun came up
somewhere east of Eden.

Dunderry Park

Poplars stand poker straight
and silver as the light would have been
bouncing off spears

two millennia ago. Those carriers
were Fianna, warriors who ran
the length of the coast

to defend territories from invaders.
I see them with their hounds,
shadows flickering

through the trees. Blonde, ragged, long
hair flows and brown, matted rat ends
dart past.

Preternatural, it is only for an instant.
The oak stands alone when once
it was lost in the woods

and cattle are foddered by a red feeder,
freshly painted,
withstanding rust and frost.

When I pause by the big black gates
opening up the road inside
I dare not enter,

not in deference to the private property sign
but from foreboding of entrance
to another realm

where ancestors call me to supper,
to renunciation of worldly goods
and to communion with a universal soul.

Dowdstown House and Hinterland, 2nd Jan. 2014

Unbridled runs the river;
over rapids the bolted year,
over dams spilling thoughts
of reflection and recollection;
winter's water atop the weir.

Damp upward steps have thawed,
mossed over with age.
Only the odd berrying bird
skirts past the solemn house,
bare, wide and proud-chested.

No anglers are to be found
where the land is swamped
where the Gabhra and the Skane
have burst their banks conjoined,
swelling with frothy mane.

The photograph taken on the bridge
later reveals the uninteresting past,
the vital and vigorous present,
the untamed future
tremulous as a leaping fish.

Rivers

I never thanked the water for all that it taught me,
until now, when I remember its blessing of innocence.
Our river was the furthest getaway on the farm,
an extremity of the world where the fabled sheep dip
was the deepest part of the course.
In gaps that the cattle made we ventured down
to the vein of the earth, waded into the lifeblood
in our wellies. We laid stones across the torrent
to make a dam, relished the sight of the gushing
and the bubbling over. At the dip we threw in sticks
and chased their path, trying to be faster.
We frequently were. But we could not stop time.
At some point we came to ignore
our mother's warnings about Jack, the bogeyman
who was supposedly roaming the fields of Cloncullen,
especially when it rained, and the river was flooded.
Now I have learned that the Cloncullen River
meets the Carollstown River before joining the Dunderry
which flows into the Clady at Bective.
The Clady enters the Boyne near Dalgan where it flows
like the Amazon through the hinterland,
quiet as a serpent and its toffee surface belies its action.
When was it that our Nile shrank to a mere tributary,
a stream of adulthood? When did the world become so small?
I never knew that one day I would have crossed over
a crumbling bridge, an unreclaimable tract,
that one day I would be the echo
in the belly of the field – calling back.

Dunshaughlin, Now and Again

On Main Street, wide and welcoming, we walk,
engaged in daily routine, the buying of groceries,
a coffee-shop-stop, a commute to work on the 109,
M3 connecting once sleeping satellite to Dublin's star.

These are the fine school days of Indian Summer
of the child's treasure-trove leaves and blackberries,
of the teenager returned to uniform, a gangly swan
barely plumed learning to fly above shedding earth.

Queen Maeve of Tara arrives at harvest,
her skirt a moon-gown, from Kilmessan to Ratoath wide,
bodice cut of Slane, Navan and Trim,
a seasoned silk, a matrimony of now and then.

Peggy Murphy writes here of Derrickstown Hill,
while Tom Englishby crosses the Irish Sea in ballad,
the passage a lamentation for his Dunshaughlin,
a rowing back of black waters, a honeyed vision.

The bell of Patrick and Seachnall rings the Angelus,
day ending with clanging heard on the breeze
by Kings of Lagore tending crannóg stone, and wood
of home, Domhnach Seachlainn, a settled and holy place.

Foley's Forge relays this din of heartbeats, anvil struck,
shoed horse clip-clopping from faded farms to mart,
and colourful years, green and gold banners,
Sam Maguire a boat on the crest of a wave.

Time ebbs and flows, ripples veined in villages and lore,
exhumed in the shadow of the famine land,
footstones raised like shields across the Boyne Valley
past Norman castles, Celtic Tiger, lingering pandemic.

Hard Man

It's hard to believe the man is the boy,
the graceful ten-year-old who liked to read,
freckle-faced, green jumper and brown corduroy
trousers, strawberry blonde hair mopping his head.
It's hard to see him walking the streets now,
where has he been and where is he going?
He could pass for obese, sweat on his brow
sauntering down Canon Row, wandering.
I think he had it tough when he was young,
same old story, dad drank, alcoholic
but whatever went on remained unsung,
the child shares a Love Heart, gesture symbolic.
Yes, compassion should refill his cracked soul
that fell to the floor, never since made whole.

Anne Sexton in Galway

1996-1998

In that confessional autumn and winter
the Atlantic kicked the leaves up Newcastle
and Thomas Hynes Road until they lay
limply in the gutters, defeated dogs.

I wondered what would become of me,
so ghostlike as I walked past the college
walls with my backpack heavy and comforting
unlike the leaden ball that sought to calibrate

itself between my stomach and throat
always just grazing the heart.
Tasked with presenting an assignment on
Sexton and Plath in a tutorial,

encouraged momentarily by the visiting lecturer,
an American woman, what did I know of 'Her Kind'?
Yet, I knew of fairy-tales and nursery rhymes,
of witches and defiant women like Lady Godiva!

I knew about shame and embarrassment,
of things I whispered to myself in the dark.
Sylvia was another matter. I took her to Salthill
and embraced her stubbornness

in the face of the saving grace of ocean.
Its tidal reminder proffered a bigger picture,
soothed those burning questions, those licking flames:
Who am I? What am I doing here? Where do I belong?

I had forgotten that the city stretched beneath one night,
shimmering yellow, orange, and red from an eyrie.
More beautiful than hell, stars scorched pale faces
in rites of passage that would be the future tattooed.

John Keats' Ghost

*"I have an habitual feeling of my real life having past,
and that I am leading a posthumous existence."*

– Keats' last letter to Charles Armitage Brown, 30/11/1820

John Keats' ghost came to me
as I watched the sun set on the April day
unspooling itself in a glory of yellow.
It was strange to see him, but he said
that he remembered me from when I was
fifteen, when I recited *Ode to a Nightingale*
and those other poems in the anthology
we read for the curriculum, *Bright Star,*
La Belle Dame Sans Merci, Ode to a Grecian Urn
and *On the Sea*. He had been looking over my shoulder
when I wrote notes in pencil on the side of the page,
something about art being able to overcome
the transience of life. He said he liked that
because look at him now, a pale spectre,
while his poetry is still renowned.
Keats resembled a black and white photograph,
except he held a brimming, purple glass of wine
as he reclined against the windowsill.
I told him that I thought that it was sad
that he had died so young.
He recounted his final year, the arterial blood
of tuberculosis, the stormy journey across the Med
to Naples, the reaching of Rome too late,
the warm weather being gone and his chance to live.
I said to him when he had finished,
"John I'm sorry, it was a cruel blow,
I mean you were only twenty-five, right?
But like you said your work lives on,
your words touch and influence people."
At that he looked up and grinned.
It was a lovely grin, wide and hopeful.

He seemed to find some peace in himself
and he turned his back to me and walked
right out into the sky, into the last flares
of the sun, tapering out like a black, burnt
piece of paper. I was glad to meet him,
claimed the first silver star for us,
and wished that I always be haunted by beauty.

Mother of Pearl

or, A skin for broken things

Darkness begins to fall after four in the afternoon
so, when I leave the supermarket the streetlights
spill orange and yellow paint across the carpark.
I think of more northern places, Scandinavia
under a green and dancing aurora borealis
and Alaska where a vampire movie I'd watched
had been set. *30 Days of Night*.
It had been a dread-filled fight to keep the demons away.
        An email pings and I open my phone to read it,
a poetry submission has come through
from a young man who writes that his decisions
haunt him daily. I feel a kinship of conscience then.
He finds no port in a porous lover's embrace,
intimacy much like the moonless, immortal kiss.
I realise then that I have been dead for too long,
anaesthetised by fear and without faith, lacklustre.
        My mind is made up to be wholly myself,
this devil must abide her angel, the wired glass
of the shattering fall to earth. When you see me,
I will be self-conscious, blushing, consumed by emotion,
trembling before the leap, innocent, shy, sweet,
resilient, miraculous as a mollusc exposed,
salted daughter of the ocean, a rock crystallised by fire,
a sight I could stand myself to watch.

II. Beyond Caravaggio

"I'll Call You..."

When the leaves fall like snow
heavy with their death to the ground
and the light bounces off the rivers and lakes
in the breath of the Arctic air
Skadi's last kiss to Njord
is remembered by firelight,
a farewell by her, who loved the ice,
to him, who loved the sea.

The Etymology of the Word *Love*

Neither of you thought of discontinuity theory,
Chomsky's single mutation, the keystone
of the formation of the capacity to speak,
the blooming, beautiful red rose of origin.
Nor did you ever imagine a mother-tongue
accepted as gospel to those within inner circle,
nor a baby unable to grasp a parent's hair
in the forest as they forage beginning
to babble soothing motherese from afar,
hands made available by vocal grooming.
You certainly never thought of the Old English *lufu*,
the German *liebe* and the Gothic *liufs*.
You might however remember the slight gestures,
the inkling that something could be amiss,
the withdrawal from a hug, the turning of a back
and the unwillingness to hold hands.
Then you would realise the connectedness
between actions and words, how the body
spoke, foreshadowing what thoughts delayed.
What history caused you to perceive the world
so differently, what experiences coloured the prism,
the prism that I had perceived as sacrosanct.
Had you been lying all along or like light dispersed
was it that you chose the word in a variant hue
investing a different degree of trust
from the very beginning of our solar system?
Is it true to say that you spoke a different language?

The Lure of Love

June nights late I am transported
To a moist and primitive land
And in its jungle confronted
By strange tethering.

I am mute and robbed of my voice,
I wonder what it would be like
To come back again in another life
To learn a new language.

Our love that was the pearl cocooned
I fear is like the promise cracked
From which the butterfly goes,
Too delicate, too short lived.

The child is aborted,
The insect screaming,
The bird caged.

Under glass I am drowning.
The mind is decayed.
I am searching and swayed.

It is no good that I am held by you.
I long to open wings
Soaring far above, away!
It is that I must know
The piercing wind –
The pang of missing you
The price of freedom
That might strike me dead.

In the painting she stands –
Despite her breasts masculine,
Playing flute and charming snakes

From the undergrowth, wearing a hood,
Immersed in shadow, perhaps after all
A snake woman herself.

Here the trees are dark green and black.
Wild roses have returned wheels in time.
Beads of rains cling to grasses.
I am empty until you fill me whole as a moon.
Your warmth is in the pink of the setting sun.
Dark land this is and my heart a leaf.

* The painting, The Snake Charmer, Henri Rousseau, 1907

Mea Culpa

In the month of the crab
on the beach in Olhos D'Agua
he raises claw and scuttles
towards the slack.

Go back to the moon
I urge him silently, embrace salt,
heal in Atlantic blue or some lagoon
caught between the rocks.

To the south Africa is ominous.
Though we cannot see her dark coastline
equatorial heat reaches across
the Sahara coaxing the orange

from its evergreen as a little sun.
Everywhere there are worlds
that we are not part of. In a key ring
purchased I keep a baby scorpion.

In the month of the aspiring moon
hopes are fulfilled and dashed
like wishes carried out to sea
by the unmerciful and austere tide.

At night the fishermen come ashore,
their boats lie magnificently on dunes,
marooned as whales, where they weigh
and barter netted fish with locals and tourists.

I try to capture the crescent in the sky
by digital camera, the effect created
luminous on the water and brightening
darkness, the romantic purple haze.

There is clearly marked a thin pathway
to another time but the trail fades
and shells are left and stars are left,
glistening, glittering, mirroring each other.

Chestnuts, Paris, September '16

Dusk comes at seven,
the tower lights up, the leaves fall,
ashen flakes, snow in a globe.
Police sirens are instrumental.
Composed by shadows the night begins to bleed;
the heckler, the pickpocket, the gambler,
this swirling cauldron of ethnicity and culture
heats Quai Branly boiling beneath blacked out stars.

Morning along Quai de Grenelle chestnuts
full as bursting popcorn hearts,
small as infants, litter pavements,
fresh and shiny from their pouches,
still dewy from somnolent milk.
Here they are dawn's bountiful crop
and not sheathed jewels.

Van Gogh's stars are luminous over the Rhone,
overtures of beauty and hope in Musée D'Orsay
singing as starlight does from a distant place.
What is there to take home only these chestnuts,
born of Paris' soil, resilient and weathered?
We doubt we will be stopped going through security,
stash them in zipped pockets for October's passage.

Beyond Caravaggio

Dublin, February 2017

There it hangs, just its-dark-self,
not even spectacular and yet closer inspection
requires even closer inspection –
this fabled work, word-of-mouth enhanced,
Chinese-whispered vast, requires some undoing.
The pronouncement of its title
is the casting of a spell:

La Cattura di Cristo

He, Himself, eyes downcast,
kissed by Judas and fled by John
while lamp-bearing Peter watches on.
And you look to the soldier's arm
wrapped in polished armour,
reflective as a mirror
and grapple with your own conscience,

as the painter had contrived
in his battle with the light and the dark.
The greatest betrayal is a watermark,
a watershed, a benchmark.
I remember the day she placed
the sword in my side, how the wound
could only heal with time and plenty of it.

Digital Shadow

You were Tyris Flare in *Golden Axe*
on the Sega and Princess Peach
in Nintendo's *Super Mario Bros.*
I might have drawn you matchstick-like
in paint on the Apple Macintosh in school
and I certainly grew to idolise your
Lara Croft form in *Tomb Raider.*

And then you were more immediate,
on mobile, I could enter chat rooms
and speak at last with you.
I devised patterns of text to let you know
I was sending you a)))HUG(((

We argued on forums, I can't even remember
what about –
but we shared luv on Bebo,
music on Myspace and you enjoyed my blog –
I lost track of you for a couple of years
but we are friends again on Facebook.

We reminisced about times past.
We'd seen the Twin Towers coming down
and the first Big Brother household.
So much water has flown under the bridge
and we know we cannot step into it twice,
that flux is a lot like creative destruction.

I've seen pictures of you on the Cloud
and we realise the prospect of a video chat.
I'd tell you how I've read reviews
of *The Emoji Movie* online,
that Rotten Tomatoes only score it 6%
but *Her* starring Joaquin Phoenix rated 95%.

Kiosk No. 6

after Banksy, Death of a Phone Booth

Before I had been the epitome
of style and technology,
classical with those communicative features,
a vermillion gentleman, dashing as Superman
and sharp as the Doctor travelling through time.

Eighty years have passed.
I can be adopted and adapted by the community
for one pound and privately owned for three thousand,
your very own curiosity, a piece of cast iron art –
or I can be cast out to the scrap yard,
a graveyard for millions of now unheard voices.

They held a public funeral for me,
my death was announced on a Soho street.
Knocked to my side and bent to an L shape,
crumpled over I bled red paint to a pool
from the pick-axe lodged in my side,
out-dated, no longer useful, void,
a footnote in the tale of I.T.'s meteoric rise.

How the West is Won

The cowboy looked like The Lone Ranger,
Billy the Kid, or Wyatt Earp,
shiny badge pinned to brown suede waistcoat,
black Stetson pointed tip down as he flung away a cigar.
Everyone wanted to be like him,
on his left hip a holster from which he pulled a silver,
heavy Colt Peacemaker, the Colt .45,
the gun that won the West.

What hope did my Sioux friend have,
his long raven hair blowing on the prairie?
He carried a tomahawk on his belt,
a bow and arrow slung across his back.
He wore feathers in his hair, ate hunted
buffalo and wore buffalo hide in winter.
The wolf ran with him under the full moon,
the fish in the streams came to the softness of his hands.

After Visiting the Hugh Lane Gallery

Dublin, November 2018

My heart is a bird's breast pierced by lilies,
my blood is the gilded gold of beauty.
Across the terrifying chaos of life,
the chasm of Bacon's scream
with his *Figure with Raised Arm*
dancing through past, present and future,
I go, tentatively, as on a tightrope
tumbling out onto the LUAS tracks of O'Connell St.,

framed in a shot of The Spire that rises up and up and up
from The Garden of Remembrance where earthbound,
turned-to-stone swans sit, The Children of Lir,
Manannán mac Lir, son of the sea, god of the mists.
For hours I am as seasick as the trapped cortege
in Courbet's *The Diligence in the Snow*.
My heart is a bird's breast pierced by lilies,
my blood is the gilded gold of beauty.

I long to run across the moors with Porphyro and Madeline
trapped in glass and verse on *The Eve of St. Agnes,*
though a rainbow may grace cloud and rooftop,
bronze leaf and flaxen leaf adorn the city's trees.
I follow the trail of music, the nightingale's lament
of Furtive Tears up the winding stairs –
my heart is a bird's breast pierced by lilies,
my blood is the gilded gold of beauty.

* *Furtive Tears* was an exhibition of work by Niamh McCann

Lau Tzu at the Door

For over a month the crows woke us
in the dawn to the sound of tapping,
their beaks once or twice to the glass,
knocks to jolt us from dreams.

I bolted the door to death
seeing only the shadow of his wing,
the disintegrating cloak of the Morrigan
a puff of dark smoke.

I watched July become August
and the past was toppled with the crop,
mooning germs in the sun's reflection.
I could not stand to look on the fields

that I had loved for their tall splendour,
their windswept secrecy. Yet when felled
and gleaned their levelness worded how
painful endings disguise new beginnings.

Leaving Oz

for Viv

Goodbye moon upside down
at 4.30 pm and 9 am in cloudless blue sky.

Goodbye possum crawling the garden fence
and sniffling outside the sliding door.

Goodbye palm trees and other trees
that I do not know the name of, and their fruit.

Goodbye sunshine making all so clear,
drying the dew, glorious by 3 in the afternoon.

Goodbye train station and familiar stops;
Roma, Corinda, Sherwood, Oxley, Darra.

Goodbye 7-11, water bottles with 33 % less plastic,
gas pumps, cigarettes and green stripes.

Goodbye snowy white dog guarding
the master's tumbledown shack

and master with the scowling face,
with the battered blue ute.

Goodbye Woolworths, to grey bags
filled with avocado, timtams, bread, Jacobs Creek.

Goodbye to alien sounding birds waking
before the dawn, to cockatiel and kookaburra.

Goodbye to walking everywhere,
to the freedom of limbs, to runners and shorts,

to the ants on the pavement,
to the worrying life beneath the grass.

Goodbye Flower Place and the Richland's hill,
to the Thirsty Camel Store, Sports Bar and hotel.

Goodbye highway, speeding car, custom made reg.
Goodbye commercial, bustling city centre.

Goodbye Mount Coot-tha, Southbank, Inala,
Forest Lake, Wacol, Brisbane, Australia.

London

March 2010

Crowds gather as though there is something to see here
and we join the waiting, shuffle from foot
to foot, stand on our tip-toes.
The traffic has stopped and a band strikes up.

They march past and I catch a glimpse
of tall blue hats entering dark gates.
The pillars of the gates are beige and golden.
They are changing the guard at Buckingham Palace.

Cast out of heaven I sip coffee-to-go
and move on back through the green
where the daffodils have yet to bloom.
The earth is recovering from the terrible frost.

By the Marble Arch a blue horse's head
points - nose down. Across the way
on a traffic island too many hangings take place.
By wagon the intended travel shackled.

When Big Ben sounds one it is clear that the town
is centre of a present world.
Its history stretches back and forth
to empire and colonies far flung.

The Thames delivers a bracing wind
along Millennium Bridge.
Past the Tower in fiction I join
Virginia on the frozen river

where Orlando skates after an exotic lover.
It was a decade ago that she went wildly
passing from arm to arm, free as thought
on the wing of youth in the night.

Picasso resides in the Tate Modern with Bacon
who pushes people out through his pictures.
They leave a snail's trail, an agony.
I will never be the same again.

In the postcard of Covent Garden evening, we dine
while underground and streets are crammed.
Later in Soho drinking doubles something
of the emigrant's life pricks conscience.

The Fish

after Elizabeth Bishop

Fragile as a rainbow,
silvery, iridescent she cannot be caught.
Some say she is the mother of the salmon run
and some say she goes with them
only to remember,
afraid that one day she could forget
the stream of consciousness she came from.

It's not enough to say that she got lost
or that she found herself lost
and yet she did find herself when she was lost,
out in the wilderness of the vast ocean
panicked and spluttering in the shock of its depth
(this the same woman who had walked along the pier
daring the engorged waves to sweep her away.
My God I had thought remembering the vision
of *The French Lieutenant's Woman*).

Stunned by the wideness of the world
she stayed in it for years, alabaster in the moonlight,
perfectly still in the starlight,
unnoticed with briny, lifeless eyes.
About her whale song and in the distance dancing light –
the beauty drove her almost mad eventually,
cracked, hatching from herself.

From birth she had strayed from an essential part,
some missing connection, a clawing sense of loss,
hungering for the elements,
bouncing from one broken bank to another.
Who could hold or feed such a creature?
The pearl in the mollusc could not sustain her
and certainly not I, thought offering my innards.

Now that she has swallowed herself
from meeting herself on the journey back
she does not thrash and flail on the line.
It would do me no good to keep her.
I had too late known that she should swim
between the sun and rain in the spray of a dream
keeping her skin.

Molly Bloom as Orlando

i. Belvedere House, 30th August 2020

Vein of woodland the stream rushes
beneath bridges and in mini waterfalls
fairy storms under lily pads
to the gold bottomed lake

on the radio Edna O'Brien had said
Joyce's writing of me showed
all great artists and James Joyce was
are androgynous, they are man and woman

this Sunday morning the world is genderless
though there are male and female joggers
and walkers in the park the autumn
sunlight offers a sort of blindness

and nature its immunity lapping water
trance inducing in this first flush of day
serotonin boosting exercise most welcome
and the unified healing of blue and green

ii. O'Connell Street, 25th May 2022

Under construction Luas tracks
spark glinting sunlight prospect-forged
in this present beneath millennium spire
gateways to travel unmapped miles

bladed chords of communication
that transmit the future perfect tense
more hi-tech vernacular thy will be done
and synonyms of expression

confused by the road works

I am taken to a standstill
rethink, rewrite, reroute –
I turn the app off and rely

on my own sense of direction
walking in black and white
as Ulysses solely along tram lines
to where the sea lashes rock –

forthcoming I watch myself
right now through memories
as if I am a great novel being written
or a work in progress fragmented

Word for Mobile

or A Sisyphean Task

As I pass a cauldron of leaf-filled puddle
splatters of heavy raindrops from trees
create muddy browns, rivulets on roads.
Wiping my rain-packed glasses with tissue, the sleeve of my shirt
post firework, post Púca procession, post trick or treat is my post-modern
morning in which I curse myself for not taking an umbrella
on the stroll through the deserted village (tagging Oliver #Goldsmith).

On a reaped field sits a two-storey of straw.
The mist lessens, perhaps the brollie was not necessary after all
(Quiet Prufrock). Breakfast hovers like a mirage in the distance;
steaming coffee, eggs poaching, simmering with salt,
maybe sausage grilled, please don't just think of pork, we have vegan
options.
The gunshot pops, or is it a leftover banger, has hunting season started?
(Postscript cock pheasant can be shot from November 1st)

What I began writing was dreamlike, caught as a dawn is.
Now I am more consciously myself, stripped in the walk, present.
This Samsung Galaxy screens sparkles with a glittering of moisture
and I will be two poems richer tapping out thoughts.
A Rottweiler and a Boxer kick up a fuss,
their fence beaded by a downpour of pearls.
Soon the tree I love appears, that holds itself
like a dancer, poised, elegant
reminds me of the physical body, the slimmer body
that I strive to achieve, the goal corporeal
a stereotype, a societal norm, who cares?
It's why I joined Weight Watchers.
I'm often accompanied by *Girl, Woman, Other* on Audible,
the joint Booker Prize winner, love it,

the interlaced stories of marginalised women
by Bernardine Evaristo (Atwood is still a queen).
Now where was I, ah yes, breakfast soon,
as soon as I change these wet socks and shoes.
At the top of the hill, I click share, email myself this document
to download to edit later, formulate lastly that if a poem
is a prison then I am a prisoner constantly breaking free.

The Colossus

I shall never get you put together entirely...

        The Colossus, Sylvia Plath

"Justice," says the sea, "is blind, comes rolling
gently today, in and out like a panting dog's tongue,
lopsided, lazy, languid." Another draft version
of itself lies on horizon where the sky meeting
is white, blank parchment, this overcast eve
on eastern Irish coast, temperate, mild.

I do not know that it will do, this split-shell,
sand-crunch-underfoot-life but somehow, it does,
inhaling deeply of seaweed, salt-spiked air.
There is a promise of summer breeze, teasing
secrecy on its wings which the gulls realise.
How they screech eagerly with piping beaks.

In the mountainous distance she awakens,
ginormous as Liberty stepping foot off her island
in Manhattan, out into the Atlantic, alarmingly.
She kicks up sludges of water from her knees,
causing quite a stir. Godzilla floundering.
She is reaching for us all. Arisen from her chair.

But now the sand grows here heavy behind damming rocks,
a wall where water under flows, as if it could be ever stopped,
and there is peace and there is trance in the order of ways,
the lost sword is returned, "tide" its double-edged word.
Swirling in an ebb and flow, a stop motion, shot of time,
dusk will fall, all in all, the Lady weighs the scales.

I am rich because I own seashells newly washed,
thrown up on the strand, gurgled up from the laughing belly
of the goddess. But as it darkens little crab you must scuttle
out to what foamy fingers she reaches to grasp you with.
It will be there on windswept dunes, matted yellow and green
with bush, that danger will come, a cloud across the moon.

Love Letter

How can the dead be dead when everything
is so alive? Waken from the dark tomb
the souls of these departed, sleeping
separated shadows in the cold room.
How wonderful it is to lift dull eyes
to the landscape and on hazed horizon
glimpse explosions of the powder pink skies,
the cherry blossom fanfare of season.
Buds grow fat as fists, cocoons fly open,
bees slumber but a while on the flower,
queens of the meadow, may's drunken titan,
skirting the dandelion, time's clock tower.
Dear Sun I love you, please stay, yours truly,
everything that grows (madly and deeply).

Matryoshka Doll

From the Marilyn Monroe lunchbox
kept under the bed (X marks the spot)
as a treasure chest, a desert island away,
she takes another case containing chains
entangled in each other from years
of neglect and lack of occasion.

Two silver strands knotted together
hold green jade and blue topaz pendants,
which she works on meticulously for a half hour
before they joyously unfurl into singularities,
unleashing memories from her twenties,
nightclubs, dinners, girls dressed up to the nines.

Using Brasso, kitchen towel and an anti-mist
cloth she polishes up the necklaces, the blackness
comes away as shadows of remaining sparkle:
the laughter of nymphs in sunshine, a child
splashing out water on a shore, an unknown
Djinn with rings on her fingers, bells on her toes.

Found Poem

Graffitied on the alleyway
that we may, or may not
have ran down as children:

Trust the universe; the sea,
the waltzing waves,
the night!

Across the depths a boat
poised between the sky and water
skimming some kind of eternity

not some dead end or cul de sac.

The Resonance of Shells

Laytown Strand, Co. Meath

Each one is singing to me, chiming in the wind;
cockle, mussel, razor and scallop. I join them urchin-like.
The sea is rushing in after being out for years,
(They are excited, excited, excited)
racing in, claiming mouthfuls of sand
that is spattered with wide, red and orange jellyfish,
the guts of the sea, supernovas.
Expectant pools join the incoming tide, embracing feverishly.
In the distance the water is sparkling emerald.

Walking the strand mauve, pink, orange, and white shingles
crunch under foot. I suppose this is leisure-taking,
a blue sky being caressed by feathered cloud,
oiled by the light of the sun.
The shells remember to tremble, anticipate the old love,
the consuming act of being, the wanting to be held
and the wholeness of water. Is it wrong to save a conch?
To imagine a future with you in it?
To listen to the timbre later and to dream?

The Singing Lighthouse

She recounts dark nights on the bay
when waves imitated the mountains,
when metal was tested and her eye
sought and fought to receive or give light –
life set as tenet in stone foundation.

Men and women in yellow jackets are versed,
orange buoys, dark inflections of fate,
crumbling walls, gestures of hope,
and despair.

And she almost whispers of the day's calm beauty,
its bewitching deception in green expanse of water,
rainbow shelled shores, the sun and its shadow
smiling and frowning on the island in the distance,
of how nature is so handsome
he can take your breath away.

Poet in a Train Station Bar

I come across you unexpectedly
as you sit, hidden behind the stairwell,
typing on your laptop.
I have walked onto a film set
where paper doors are punched through
or sliced to reveal their artificiality,
or into a hall of mirrors.
I am not sure which reflection is real.

I do not believe you have noticed me.
I choose to sit very far away
and I wonder what it is you are writing,
so clean-cut and groomed, a winner,
a man who takes himself seriously,
comfortable in your own skin
but with something renegade attached,
a note to your childhood perhaps,

or a slighted card dealt driving
frightful ambition, a Scarlet Pimpernel
or Count of Monte Cristo lost
to this Parisian place now,
sailing past rugged Gallic coast
the bow crashing up and down
on swelling water as you gaze,
knowingly, to horizon.

I digress, look up from newspaper headlines,
catch the back of a figure leaving
through darkened doors. I doubt
anyone has traversed the furthest corners of you,
your hankering for the wild and solitary places,
disappeared, known only to God
in this nameless humanity
where we struggle for connection.

Millionfold

In the back seat of the car, she lists out
numbers higher than the sky, a million,
a trillion, a zillion, letters without
the weight of their quantity, a squillion!
Perhaps she is building a skyscraper
in her head to match the height of those words,
or painting giraffes above pink clouds,
or planning to fly a kite of paper?
Each child asks what the biggest number is,
agreeing in time on infinity
learning of its meaning and the power
of knowledge, its imparting chivalry.
What starts out small divides and multiplies
grows and strengthens, a sun that never dies.

Researching Thomas Hardy

for Sarah

It's a midnight wire for help, a scouting
for information about the writer.
She's driving down to Max Gate, hoping
to wing it on her route to Dorchester.
How do you document his life on screen,
extricate his bones from the paper's page?
Who had brave Tess of the D'Urbervilles been,
is she a relic from a different age?
I follow her on the hard pagan earth
misused, loved, rejected, many women
hide beneath her voluminous brown skirt,
coat the dagger she drives with cinnamon.
And then the dim hope of *The Darkling Thrush* –
I picture my friend, the camera her brush.

Sevilla

Silently I am looking for the hidden Moor
through glass watch him peering darkly from a passage way
cut in the cliff's face. It is on old Spain we stare
in our carriages, rocked back - and forth, to present day.

They write about "El fuego" in the newspaper, great fire
having taken grip in the East and in Madrid.
I see smoke everywhere as memories rekindling desire.
It is thirty seven degrees in the city as beads gather on my forehead.

We pass the bullring going to Plaza De Arnas, pay the fare,
but there blood gushing from his taurean body dust in trail,
matador poised in tension struts in gold encrusted armour.
Later they dance Flamenco in this frying pan Seville.

Leaving at half past six it is still, dark, in the morning sleeping
in tangerine streets of burnt spice before the sun an orange rising.

The Tinder Stick Road

Do not expect the way to be easy,
that branches will not sharpen like knives,
that thorns will not adorn the middle ground.
From a past you no longer serve
be free. Set one naked sole after another
on the coals until they are doused.

Imagine the end, all the little endings
of the journey, the daily living.
Imagine that comfort in the hold of the rose,
the soft pink, and red, petals and folds.
Did any voyage ever begin with certainty?
Not Ithaka! Not Bethlehem! Not Jerusalem!

Look to the stars, to Polaris and Orion.
Never be dissuaded, so that they may orbit you
when seeking them in the glittering beyond.
Let the heavens swarm like bees in the godlike centre
of your existence, your heart writing clefs and quavers
in love for yourself, this life, this humanity.

What Became of the Horses

after Michael Longley's The Horses

Imagining the fall of Patroclus,
and with the spent rage of Achilles
still haunted by those ashen features,

I am walking past the faded stables
that lie in deep green fields, by sleeping castles,
the main gates stripped of paint.

The animals kept were promises and dreams
defeated in battles by hardships and losses,
beaten down, their spirits depleted.

Above the red-brick pillars of the entrance
to history the leaves of a copper beech stir.
Xanthos and Balios are awakened by their father

the West Wind, their distant hoofbeats disturb
the ants, make the wild rose tremble,
this softest rustling is enough to soothe a jaded heart,

I like to think they gallop through eternity,
that they can be summoned by those in need,
their tears, stellar ointment to the wounded.

Windswept

Windswept birds, windswept wings,
windswept trees, windswept grass,
windswept moon,

halved –

windswept hair, windswept breeze,
whistling, shaking nests.
Windswept hands of the clock.

Windswept voiceless being,
being without form, windswept,
painting the world with thoughts,
making the world

{{{{{windswept}}}}}

Word Skin

They have seeped into me
invisible dyes that will never leave.
Washing in the river they are the river;
the bank, the froth, the rock, the pebble,
the reeds, the gurgle, the swish, the fish,
the cormorant, the heron,
the roc – a passage of Sartre on the rapids,
Goethe's sorrow in driftwood,
the protracted silence between gongs of the bell.

I saw an otter sluiced in water
sleek as a seal silky with sunlight
diving and twisting as an eel
and he had the same skin.
Searching in the darkness, the submarine,
knowledge is an impression
a cloud-like fog clearing, a day-dream,
a knowing without knowing how or why
an instinctive mastery.

And there you are...

Clashes of will, miscommunication,
this history of crossed swords,
make messy ingredients for any kind of match!

Yet there you are, always ready
to offer a hand when she is fallen,
children in a playground.

There you are when she looks inward,
for inspiration and some straight to the point,
no-holds-barred truth.

Someone who offers friendship,
whose gifts you are unsure still of accepting,
a foil to excesses, a questioning of soul,

a relationship that withstands time.
A great love to come, or a self, actualised,
one whom you cannot be without –

is that what our paths crossing has been about?

Amelia Earhart Reaches Ireland, Earns her Wings

21st May 1932

Somewhere near Howland Island in the Pacific Ocean
the Queen of the Air and navigator Noonan,
plunged, forever phantoms of sky, ghosts of the deep.

Before, from Newfoundland, she had aimed for Paris.
The bright red Lockheed Vega 5B
landed instead, almost fifteen hours later,
in Gallagher's green pasture, Derry, Northern Ireland.

I picture her in leather jacket, hair cropped,
cap and goggles on, machine a streak of crimson phoenix,
cruising comet over white, then grey clouds.
She fiddles with gauges and dials, sips tomato juice,
spies shoreland in the far distance, an Emerald Isle.

Just a little further, she whispers. *Just a little further.*

ORLA FAY is the Poetry Ireland Town Laureate for Dunshaughlin, County Meath. For this initiative between Poetry Ireland and Meath County Council Arts Office she was commissioned to write "Dunshaughlin, Now and Again". In September 2018 she had a winning poem in Hennessy New Irish Writing in The Irish Times. In 2019 she was longlisted for The Anthony Cronin International Poetry Prize, shortlisted for The Cúirt New Writing Prize, The Bailieborough Poetry Prize, The Francis Ledwidge Poetry Award and won 3rd Prize in The Oliver Goldsmith Poetry Award. In 2020 she won 3rd prize in The Jonathan Swift Creative Writing Award. In 2022 she won Fingal Libraries: Travels with Joyce Poetry Competition. In 2018 she completed a MA in Digital Arts and Humanities at UCC where she wrote a thesis on Poetry in the Digital Age. Her poem "What Became of the Horses (after Michael Longley's 'The Horses')" was included in The Ireland Chair of Poetry Commemorative Anthology, *Hold Open the Door*, published by UCD Press. She has published two chapbooks, *Drawn to the Light* and *What Became of the Horses*. She edited *Boyne Berries* from 2014 to 2021. She launched an online magazine of poetry, *Drawn to the Light Press* in October 2020. She has been the recipient of a professional artist development bursary from Meath County Council Arts Office, and an agility award from the Arts Council of Ireland.

salmonpoetry

Cliffs of Moher, County Clare, Ireland

"Publishing the finest Irish and international literature."
Michael D. Higgins, President of Ireland